MIRRAN THOUGHT

1

MIRRAN THOUGHT
Spitzwiesenstr. 50
90765 Fürth
Germany

www.dwmirran.de
www.empty.de
empty@empty.de

Read Twentythree (MT-628)

Print and publication by BOD
In de Tarpen 42
D-22848 Norderstedt
www.bod.de
nfo@bod.de

First printing 2020
ISBN: 978-3-7519-7068-6

MIRRAN THOUGHT is the publishing arm of Mirran Threat, a company devoted to releasing the music and writings of the various members of Doc Wör Mirran. Mirran Thought and Mirran Threat are both divisions of MT Undertainment.

BROKEN

Joseph B. Raimond

Written in Fürth Germany from 2008
to 2011. Drawings 2008 to 2020.

Cover art: "Adolation" Joseph B.
Raimond 2020

As always, in loving memory of
Frank Abendroth and Tom Murphy.

For Conny, my perfect angel

Dedicated to George Floyd

This is DWM release Nr. 177

Frieda Envy

Frieda the common housefly
so dumb, so disgusting
what do you expect from a former maggot?

With six legs and two wings
god knows how many eyes
so many muscles in perfect harmony
precision defines her flight
and
it's just not fair!

Peacemeal

Patience is such an incredible virtue sometimes
when the fists fly and I have to keep myself busy
turning the other cheek

Waiting, waiting, waiting,
while my blood boils and my eyes see red
someday my day will come
the light will shine on my soul
and
I will finally know freedom

Homeless Hopeless

Give me the dirty, damp alley artist
with dirty, work-worn fingers and a tear in his eye
for he is the one true poet

Bottom dwelling slime as paint, or perhaps ink
As alcohol and drugs lubricate the brain
To create wonders that inspire the uninspired
But don't look him in the eye
and
just pretend he's not there

Rusted Frame

This schitzophrenic business
smiley, smiley, smiley, and a shit faced grin
only hides the rot inside

Peel the skin and set the stench free
just dig below the shiney surface a bit
and expose the rusted frame
How can you take so much
and
give so little?

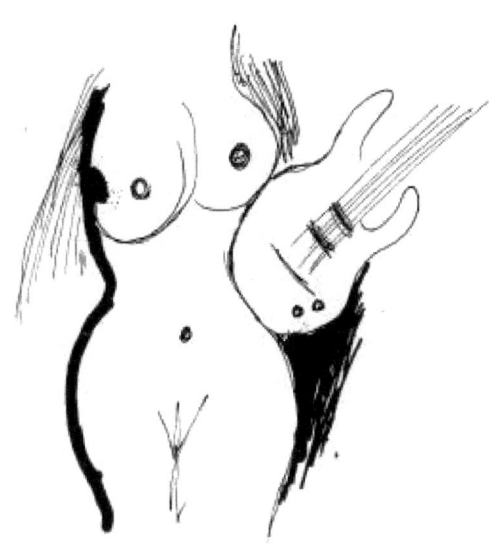

<u>Champ Anja</u>

After so many years, I'm on her map!
not the center of town
but at least within her city limits

Always in elegance, a gaze up to her
her stage a modern pedestal
the wind of eternity
whisping through her long black hair
and
around the beauty of her fine, graceful figure

Infinity Beckons

Down, down, down
rubbing my face in the dirt
like the wart on a dead mole's nose

Even the blues is a color
when you see everything in a tone of grey
for all is relative
when down is forever
and
infinity beckons

<u>Flirting 101</u>

You're giving me the eye
Fine by me
So I'll give you the eye back

Not bad for her age, so
Let's skip all the preliminaries
Forget what we learned in flirting 101
We're not getting any younger
and
The light at the tunnel is getting brighter

Snuggle Industrial

So cold, snuggle in your covers
the secret side to every
hardcore industrial, hate inspired musician

Hard as steel, cold blooded
Nazi insignia collectors
just want to sleep late, clouds in my coffee
quick kiss on the door out to work
and
dream of your next release

Entrenched

So old, entrenched
in the middle age
always looking back, but hurled into the future

Without a doubt, scared, blood runs cold
at the thought of
blood, needles, failing organs
young doctors and pretty nurses
and
they are all staring at my naked ass

<u>Sicko</u>

Sort of jam, man
lets get pop with a little aggro
just to be able to stay even a little cool

I'll keep my mouth shut
all these years
brood, brood, talk bad about you
behind your back at every chance I get,
and
be a sicko to you when you are nice

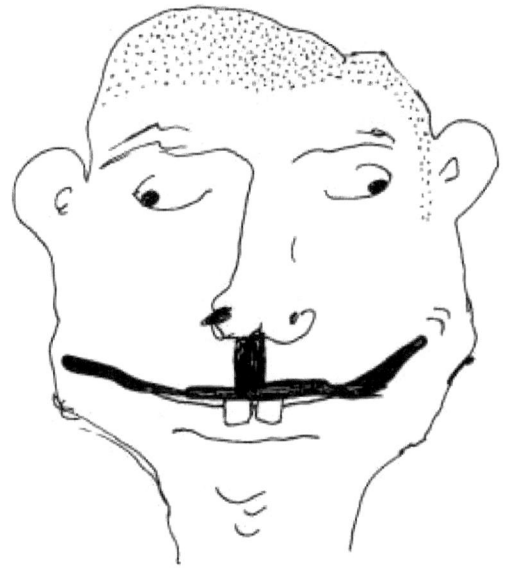

Absurdicus

Stand among your Roman,
pseudo-columns
and proclaim your duty to the people

We have heard your shallow arguments
your hollow lies
those of us that think see you for what you are
the power hungry emperor, that can barely read
and
perpetually grins like any other mindless smiley face

<u>Safety Pins</u>

One two, FUCK YOU!
jam, man, fast hot and sweaty
like it should and always will be

We are gonna slam, fast and furious
define the punk
as the highest possible, purest form of culture
a zenith, perpetual goal
and
final destination of every Frank Sinatra and Elvis

Plummet To Man

Fall, falling forever
man as object of hate, forever
plummet to depths where no man has gone before

Nothing can save mankind
from his own greed, hate, ugliness
there is no hope, there never was hope, ever
we just need to realize this
and
prepare for impact

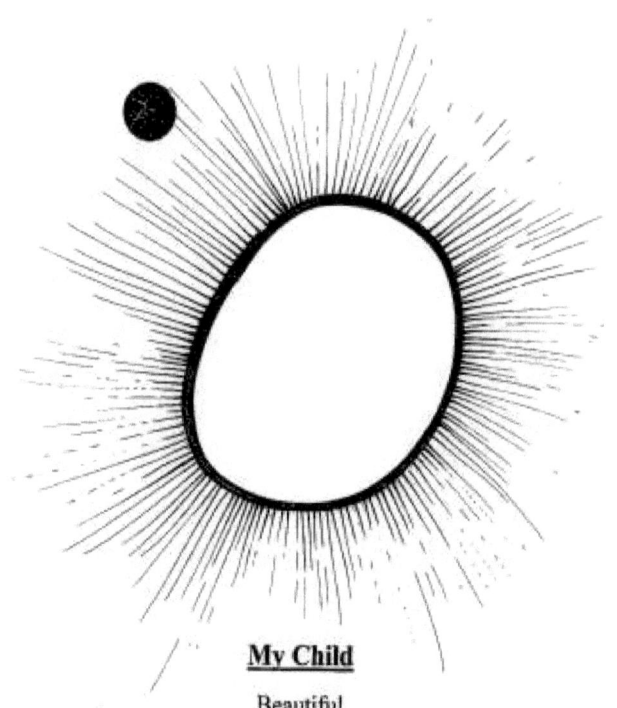

<u>My Child</u>

Beautiful
a gift to the world,
regardless of what you accomplish or you become

Nothing can shake nor diminish
my love for you
for ever, I will be there for you
just, let me into your heart
and
forget what other people say

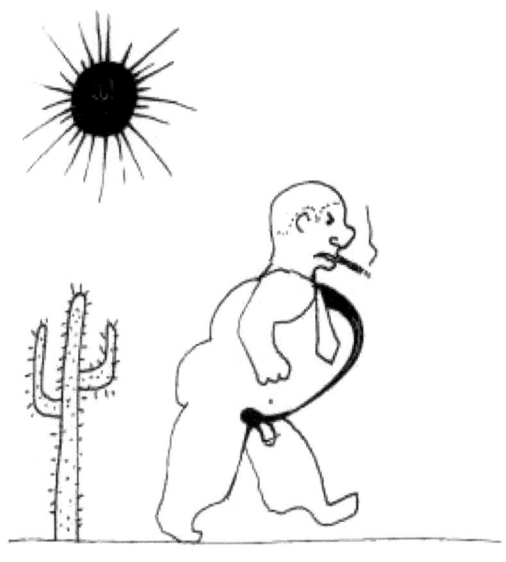

Excuse

My daily routine,
a prison from which
I am forever trying to escape

I have banished employment, complete
with tyrant boss, sent to the dessert
but routine has filled that void, and
I have just as little time left as ever before
and
this is why I just don't have the time to help you now

Musty

That musty smell,
reminds, brings back vivid memories
of what seems like centuries past

Skipping off with a beer, hoping not to get seen
by the fat man, who later died, sad
of first time sex, innocent and naive,
with dreams invading our thoughts
and
a love for this world, not yet spoiled by reality

Dead And Gone

Every last one of them, gone
to leave me behind, aimless
to ask each one "are you my momma?"

They grew old, tired
and I never forgave them for that
just plain mean of them you know,
to get all wrinkled in their wisdom, then leave me
and
all my uncertainties, intact

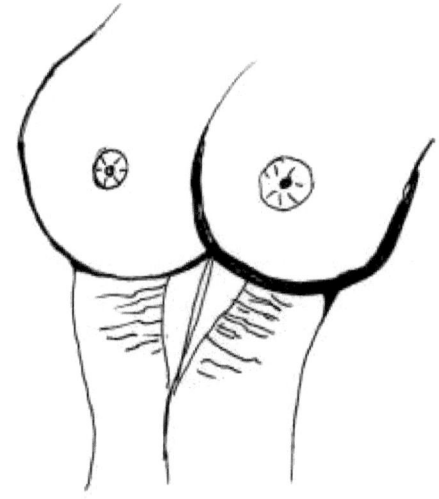

Fine

I don't want to fuck you,
I just wanna fuck you
I don't want to screw you, I just wanna screw you

Fuck me, are you fine
an object you say? but what is wrong with that?
shape and form,
beauty and color, it's how we define art
and
how I define your body

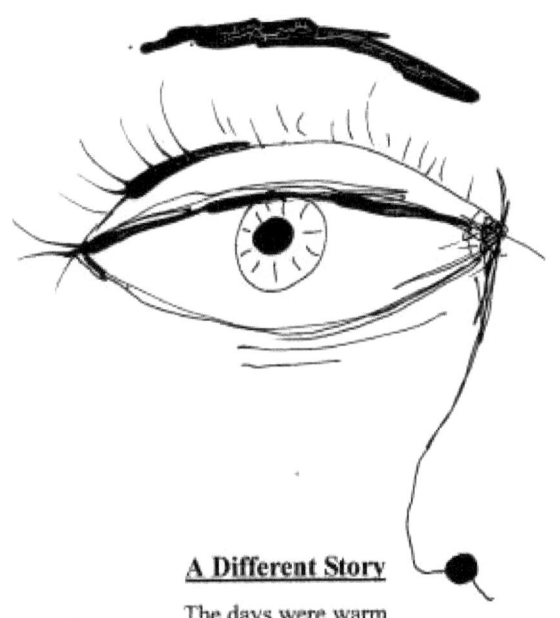

A Different Story

The days were warm
our time, endless
we had all the world could offer

The beer was cold, the sex was easy
our only concern, will mom smell the stale smoke?
the party seemed long,
but in the end, was only the blink of an eye
and
now my wrinkles hint of a different story

Stunned

I walk, daily routine that never changes
through the wild, wilderness of green, sunshine
but am bothered by trains, am blind to beauty

The world passes, and I fit less and less
always running behind, trying to catch up to a
something that everyone says
is on sale now, don't be a schmuck and miss out
and
let your own kids be ashamed of you

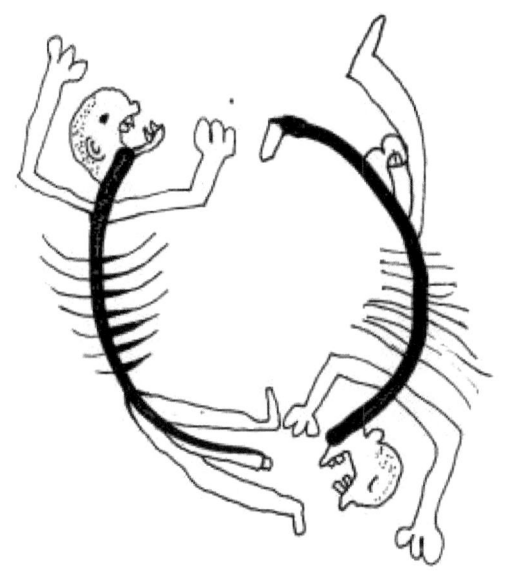

My Personal Catch 22

My bones are turning brittle, I can tell
they squeek at the joints and stiffen
my muscles ache as if I had worked out, stupid idea

My brain is rusting of routine, my mind
always slipping into meaningless daydreams
of revenge fantasies against former friends and bureaucrats
both mind and body are in a perpetual contest
and
both are gaining speed, but neither is winning

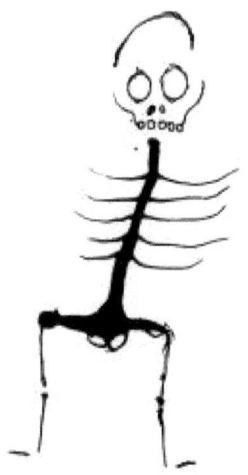

<u>Thinner</u>

Life is thinning with age,
my blood, mixed with alcohol,
my patience for you

My art, spread out between too many dreams
my wallet, as my women feel free to help themselves
my mind, as age's confusion is welcomed in my thoughts
only my hair is bucking this trend, so far at least
and
my waist, allies in thicker

My House

This is my house
not your house, not his house
not even her house

It's mine, all mine, and you can't have any
a hypocritical anarchist, you say? perhaps
I see it as a refuge though
free of bureaucrats
and
governed by mutual respect

Home

The saying goes:
"you can't go home again"
how painfully, arrogantly, totally true

I attempt to see the place with new eyes,
but the bliss of rememberance: there was my first kiss,
a long walk home in the snow after my first beer buzz,
long dead friends, young naive love
and
those endless summer days, and I am again blind

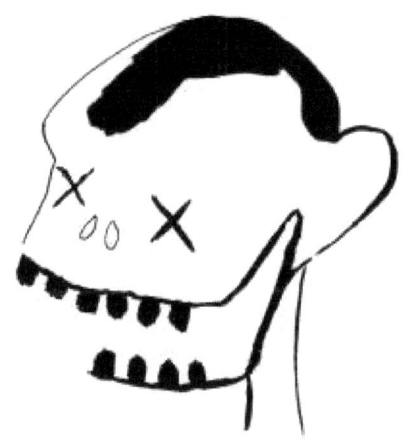

Cure My Haunts

Cure my haunts,
my fears, pains and doubts
with what the future will bring

Freeze me,
in a perpetual sleep, safe from age
forever, if need be, free from the
disease of my mind
and
the disease we call our modern society

<u>Scapegoat Joe</u>

When the going gets tough,
the tough vote for the wrong candidate
time, and time again

I don't appove of your police state politics,
policy to interpret the world
according to your national interests, only
and leave me and my children, exposed to revenge
and
hate, as everyone's scapegoat

Linus, My Cat

Partners in crime,
partners in being ignored
you and I have a lot in common

Set out in the elements, we must endure
a home that is always cold and unloving
always in the way with a sharp word
a swift kick with no remorse, my ally
and
only friend

<u>What Have We Become?</u>

In so many years
a routine of indifference has been set in stone
unbreakable, hopeless, stable as time forever

When you no longer call me sweetie
when that spark has left your eyes
when you no longer leave me little love notes
when I get home late from work
and
I can see that you are not glad to see me

Partner

A partner in crime, a partner for life?
Hah!
You're not even a partner in cards

Flying fists are not an ingredient
of even a half-baked love
making sure I feel like shit
day for day for day
and
the loneliness of a married night

<u>For Frank, Again</u>

Where are you when I need you?
You left me here, without warning
How dare you die without saying goodbye first, true friend

A subtle joint, you always had the best
a dream of unhampered creativity
inspired by a healthy dose of hatred for bureaucrats
you mixed this all together with your amazing
and
boundless intelligence, so lets jam!

Bleed, But

I'm bleeding, but you don't care
I'm dying inside, but you don't notice
I'm so lonely, but you're not at my side

I'm so afraid sometimes, but you're out shopping
I'm mad at what you did, but it's never your fault
I'm searching for answers, but you endlessly nag at me
I'm trying to explain, but you don't listen
and
I'm getting sick of all these "buts"

<u>Ben</u>

You're gonna say "oh, man!"
but Ben, you have become our Syd Barrett
our legend of an almost rock star

Your own worst enemy, promises shouted
a little bit of creativity,
finally laid to rest
for a little bit of security
and
a shit job in the oral hygiene department of a walm-art world

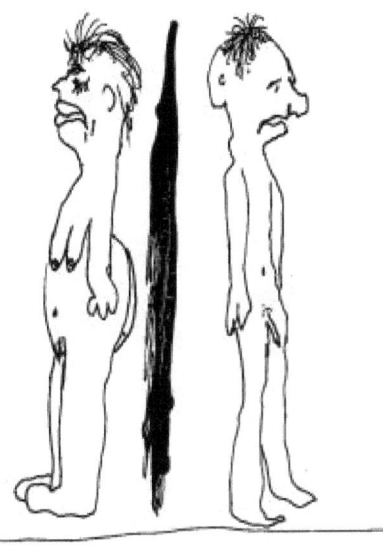

Rot

Denial, always, from the beginning
"it will never happen to us"
we thought we were immune

It came creeping, inevitable, at a snail's pace
before we even noticed,
it was too late, we were infected
the game of indifference, boredom
and
routine had just begun

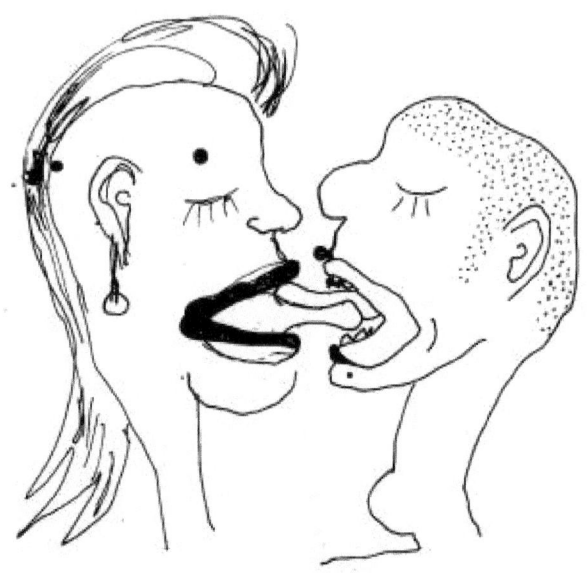

Lay Luck

Lay luck, make her happy
bring her to heights, unknown to groan
so she will forever look for you in her dreams

Lay luck, keep her satisfied
a gleam in her eye when she thinks of you
ready to give you insider news
an edge over the others
and
no one will suspect

Stone Cold

Will I ever lay forever, next to you, or without?
thoughtless routine of future generations to ignore me
someday, dug up, then discarded

I only know, I am tired of being in the center ring
a plaything for fate, or some other female tyrant
no one to answer my questions
no one to look me in the eye
and
let me be a little boy again

Hero

Let me be your hero
the one you look up to
the one that tells you where to go

Let me be your hero
offering wisdom and understanding
when you just don't fit in, and nobody cares
I want to inspire you to greatness
and
bring you to yourself

A Perfect Fear

Is the one that just doesn't let go
lets your knees start giving, weak
shakes you in your bones

Can't sleep at night, dreams are all mixed
distorted and amplified, fevered like sickness
wake with a fright,
a shake, sweat covered
and
a scream fighting to emerge

Bleak

The days are short and grey
there's a depression that hangs like a sadness
through the eyes of everyone you meet

The times are changing,
optimism has died a slow and painful death
as a grim uncertainty has invaded the land
with a fear of what the future could bring
and
a sadness that swims in the well of despair

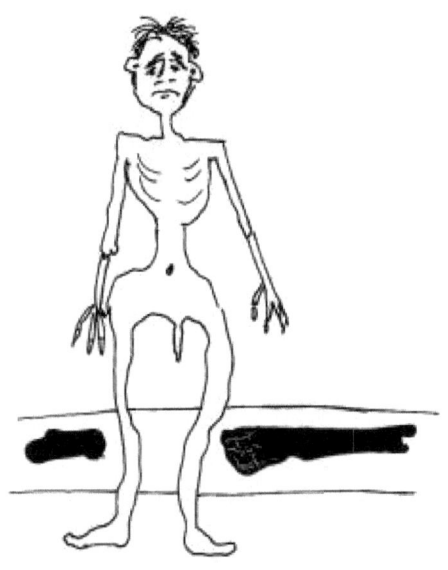

Broken

My body, breaking, slowly
through the years, nodding towards elderly
is giving up on me, jumping ship

Dragging my mind, my love of life
down with it, time isn't on my side
so with what little enthusiasm I can muster,
I get up, day after day
and
try to pretend that the young pretty girl winked at me

Detached

Slowly, easing my way towards breakdown
pushing everyone and everything out of the way
to make way for nothing

Black, my state of mind, but getting
used to it
I can't remember the warmth of the sun,
the kiss of my lover
and
the look of love in anyone's eyes

Tyrant

Boss of the world, my world
control every move I make, every breath I take
nothing goes without your approval

I'm not allowed my own thoughts
even the brief look of independent thought in my eyes
brings cries of protest,
accusations of disinterest
and
the fear that you no longer control me

<u>Penetraitor</u>

We will we will:
Fuck you poke you stroke you
maim you eat you beat you cheat on you

We are gonna slam, fast and furious
define the sex
as the highest possible, purest form of culture
a zenith, perpetual goal
and
final destination of every washed up punk rocker artist

Shit Hop

They prance around, cool, and think they're the shit
but their message is nothing but tits, ass and sex,
big cars made for pigs and gold round their necks

With their 15 minutes stardom, and a brief spotlight
over their arrogant, macho heads,
they could've given so much to the world, inspired our youth
but they wasted it on their ego
and
for this they can't be forgiven

Vat

A plug has come undone, reality
has returned to silence for a brief second
as the brain bathes in sensorial bliss

The technician scribbles onto his pad
makes adjustments, turns some dials
and I see colors, the lush green of the spring day
hear the bees as the fly by my ear, smell the fresh blossoms
and
I am happy in my vat

Barrage

I've strengthened my force field
like in all those old star trek episodes
to fuddle your plans of a verbal barrage

Its like an invisible bubble
that surrounds me, protects me
from the meanest of your insults,
from your tyrany and ignorant assults
and
let me tell you, its working better and better

Braggart Of Pain

Why is it that
those that bitch the most
always do the least?

I know, I know,
nobody works as hard as you
nobody is in as much pain as you
nobody has the right to be as tired as you
and
I'm such an asshole for not accepting this

Ground Pounder

Pound the ground
until you get stationed back to "the world"
If you're lucky, you won't get shot first

Right-wing brain-washers send you to foreign soils
in anticipation of doing the right thing, they say
protect your country, way of life, your flag
Which is only a lie, because in their eyes
and
heartless soul, you are expendable

Guilt Poetry

An early morning guilt poem
as a last minute substitute
for a couch potato evening the night before

As old age creeps up and rings the doorbell
you didn't spend a night on the town afterall
so you were home, no excuses there
watching TV, swilling beer
and
not giving a fuck about your art

No Authority

Don't tell me what to do, ever
not in a subtle way, not in a direct way
not in any way

I will never accept an authority
not a government, not a law, not a god, not a wife
not an opinion, not a boss,
not what the neighbors think
and
not even myself

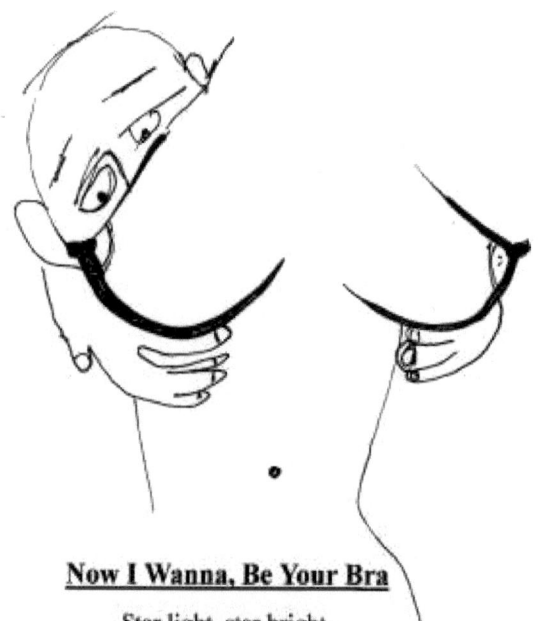

Now I Wanna, Be Your Bra

Star light, star bright,
first star I see tonight,
I wish I may, I wish I might, I wish...

I was your bra, protector of perfection
supporter of form
pink frills, black latex
a thick white cotton job, whatever you
and
your nipples prefer

Dick Extender

The prick's dick extender
an ugly, peanut brained pitbull terrier
and snarls from under a studded leash

Or is it the massive motored, chromed
hotrod to hide his little rod
set of wheels that he thinks impresses me
or her
and
will get his little peter laid?

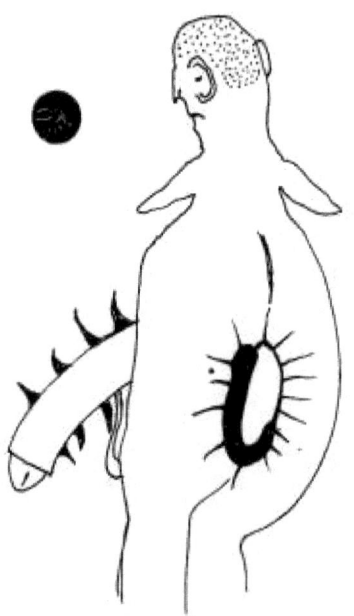

Prickle Prick

Thorny toad, horny toad
with a huge asshole,
stick to her, first your dick, then your fist

You're in a no-win situation, granted
so be careful, don't do her no wrong
look both ways when crossing the street
watchout for her brother's left, it's a killer
and
keep on treating her like shit

Humdrum

Tired of the humdrum
tired of the worry
tired of the nine to five, hurry

I don't want responsibility
I don't need respectability
I don't answer to authority
I don't accept your bureaucracy
and
so I won't sign on the dotted line

Lay Luck

To bed, finger fuck
as a trade for foreskin
foreplay, your wish is my command, studly

I'll take a house of wood, thank you
to house my love
a million dollars to work for me,
slave driver of dough
and
inspiration

Death VIP

It is springtime
everyone else is falling in love
but I only fall out of love

The days are long
but my patience is short
the sun is bright
but my mood is dark
and
my time is running out

Sinister Nose

A big fuzzy bumblebee
buzzing round my nose
quite an achievement in itself, actually

Looking for a sweet, springtime flower
does he realize how far off the mark he is?
for what could be darker, uglier
moodier
and
more sinister than what is behind this nose?

Rockstar Dreams

Digging his own grave,
rockstar old age, getting ready for death
he just turned twenty six

Lured by the spotlight, the screaming fans
faceless, nameless, genderless sex
tabloid headlines and drug induced depression
no regrets, all of it cool
and
only the prelude to this last performance

A Wench In Folds

Fed by the enthusiasm
of an artificial sun, eyes falling
deeper into her skull

A bad memory and a few faded photos
the only testimony left to tell
of her youth, so toasted and burned
the lines of age crisp, deep
and
multiplying